DREAMS FOR EARTH

Poems

Fatima-Ayan Malika Hirsi

Illustrated by Ángel Faz and Jack (Anna) Jackson

DEEP VELLUM PUBLISHING
DALLAS, TEXAS

Deep Vellum Publishing
3000 Commerce Street, Dallas, Texas 75226
deepvellum.org · @deepvellum

Deep Vellum is a 501c3 nonprofit literary arts organization founded in 2013
with the mission to bring the world into conversation through literature.

Copyright © 2025 Fatima-Ayan Malika Hirsi
Illustrations © 2025 Ángel Faz and Jack (Anna) Jackson
Edited by Sophia Terezawa

First edition, 2025
All rights reserved.

Support for this publication has been provided in part by grants from the National Endowment for the Arts, the Texas Commission on the Arts, the City of Dallas Office of Arts and Culture, the Communities Foundation of Texas, and the Addy Foundation.

Paperback ISBN: 978-1-64605-399-5
Ebook ISBN: 978-1-64605-400-8

LIBRARY OF CONGRESS CATALOGING-IN-PUBLICATION DATA

Names: Hirsi, Fatima-Ayan Malika author | Faz, Ángel illustrator | Jackson, Jack (Anna) illustrator
Title: Dreams for Earth : poems / Fatima-Ayan Malika Hirsi ; illustrated by Ángel Faz, and Jack (Anna) Jackson.
Description: Dallas, Texas : Deep Vellum, 2025.
Identifiers: LCCN 2025013393 (print) | LCCN 2025013394 (ebook) | ISBN 9781646053995 trade paperback | ISBN 9781646054008 ebook
Subjects: LCGFT: Poetry
Classification: LCC PR9199.4.H58 D74 2025 (print) | LCC PR9199.4.H58 (ebook) | DDC 811/.6--dc23/eng/20250402
LC record available at https://lccn.loc.gov/2025013393
LC ebook record available at https://lccn.loc.gov/2025013394

Cover art and design by Ángel Faz and Jack (Anna) Jackson
Interior layout and typesetting by KGT

PRINTED IN THE UNITED STATES OF AMERICA

PRAISE FOR *DREAMS FOR EARTH*

"Offering profound reflections on our past, present and future fractals, Fatima-Ayan Malika Hirsi carefully threads the needle to pinpoint articulations of a world in perpetual motion. These poems are rich with whale song, Sun Ra earthbound, sonic landscapes where the dream and the material collide to reveal how the act of creation is diurnal, ceaseless, and inevitably, our greatest asset. *DREAMS FOR EARTH* is an intimate look at the interiority of motherhood—how structures of neocolonialism and climate catastrophe shape the self and the worlds around it in various forms and fervor. This collection is a vibrant tapestry of all our various wounds and the flowers that bloom in between them."

—**Ashia Ajani, author of** *Heirloom*

"To read Fatima-Ayan Malika Hirsi's *DREAMS FOR EARTH* is to be held by an effervescent river teeming with the fury of a thousand disquieted beings. Bridging earth and sky, the poems awaken as a flock of herons circling overhead, offering searing witness to the infinite atrocity that is police violence, Zionist occupation and shattered genealogy. Amidst the mind-numbing turbulence of modernity, Fatima conjures a dreamcurrent for us to ride that sends anger earthward so we might recall how 'to absorb the sky's sermon' and 'haunt all those who dare unbraid your glory.'" —**shō yamagushiku, author of** *shima*

"*DREAMS FOR EARTH* is a strikingly visceral account of the tension between worlds: the one that is ending, the one that could've been, and the many constantly looming with every unprecedented moment. From poem to poem, Fatima-Ayan Malika Hirsi holds the reader's hand in the dark corner of a bucolic scene and evinces the felt impact of collapse as it happens simultaneously, surely, and ominously. Hirsi carefully but masterfully unveils the ways in which moments designated for joy now require us to bear the necessary weight of empathy and care, and the responsibilities we have to each other."

—**Sasha Banks, author of** *america, MINE*

"Fatima-Ayan Malika Hirsi adds her voice to poetry's sacred search for the better spells between us, conjuring names that 'do not refract / grief,' children as 'little orchestras bouncing through the streets,' and 'a taste of what's to come.' Bless this bright poet's incantatory dreaming. May we walk inside the wilderness of its safety one soon day."

—**Geffrey Davis, author of** *One Wild Word Away*

"To be honestly alive today is to experience the breadth of rage and grace that Hirsi gathers together in this courageous, moving book. Resisting empire's assaults on our shared humanity, these poems witness and face the unbearable brutality that empire has unleashed upon our kin. When it feels impossible to say anything more, Hirsi offers us much needed words to keep birthing with the world we need, the one that is possible because of yarrow, mango, ocean, olive, keffiyehs, and the medicine that grows when we reciprocate earth's gifts with love, gratitude, and attention. She reaches deep into the reserves of life that mothers conceive and tend so tenaciously, pulling up seeds, grief, songs, petals, and prayer to keep our spirits aligned with the earth." —**Rita Wong, author of** *Current, Climate*

"Courageously dedicated to the heart of what is true and necessary, these poems weave and storytell with grace and power. They will embolden you—encouraging you to imagine another shape for our world, to dream a healing, and to take action on behalf of this dream. Intentional and precise in form, these poems give us striking permission to widen, to extend. Stunningly honest, a tender reckoning, we vision and do not look away. Illustrated with magic, collaborative, and deep, this collection moves. At moments, I was called to read aloud; as chant, spell, archive, protest, prayer, narrative, eulogy, praise. Let this book accompany you in grief, rage, fear, joy, and our collective possibility."

—**Aiyana Masla, author of** *The Underdream* **and** *Stone Fruit*

For my mother, who taught me to love words.
For my children, who inspire me to dream.

Table of Contents

I.

DREAM FOR EARTH   5

WARNING   6

Seeing   7

Histories   8

Orb: Do Not Disturb   9

Ways I am Like My Mother   11

Kill the Messenger   12

YouTubes My Mom Sends Me   14

II.

Doll   19

Sick Day   21

Dallas, Before E   22

"Lost Valley is just a microcosm of the world."   24

Duplex   26

Patterns   27

Cohabitation   29

Project Yarrow   30

III.

Frequently Asked Question   33

Of Naming And Not   34

"Lost Valley is just a microcosm of the world."   36

"Lost Valley is just a microcosm of the world."   37

Orb: Dream of Earth   38

Orb: Forms of Worn Out   39

Of Rivers and Futures   40

Orb: Climate Collapse is Fucking up my Birth Plan   41

IV.

Again Birthing Again Birthed Again Again Again   45
Orb: Bloodletting   47
Inheritance   48
Tornado Sirens When You Have A Sleeping Baby   50
Hope Is A Sweet Evening Sky Ripening   53
Anticipation   56
Abecedarian Mango   57
Poem About Pockets   61
Prayers to Gentle Cat   62
Searching for Mary Oliver and Always Finding Men   64
Indoctrination   66
Ghazal for Abolition   67
An Astrology   68
They say I'm a beast.   71
Eye Gazing with Monsters   72

V.

A Cautionary Tale   77
Hubris   78
Dallas, TX 2019 / Bishop Arts Typewriter Poem for Jim about Physics   79
Victoria, B.C. 2023 / Government Street Typewriter Poem For Della About Turtles   80
August. Blackberries Everywhere.   81
Church at Prairie Fest   82
God Silence   84
Epithalamium   85
Time Simulation   87
Generational Joy   88

VI.

DREAM FOR EARTH   93
Black & White Scream   98
Solidarity   99
"This is the soul of my soul"   100

In an emergency room watching videos of Gaza   101
March 2024   104
Planting Seeds   107
Remarks by President Biden on Recent Events on College Campuses /
his truth in his lies   109
Girl, Bye (These Boots Are Made For Walking)   111
Tell the Children   112
Fecundity   113
Thresholds   115
A Threading   117
DREAM FOR EARTH   122

Notes   125
Acknowledgments   127

DREAMS FOR EARTH

DREAM FOR EARTH

Joy   the only bomb   loud plume of fuss falling into Monday
  Calypte anna gorget   crimson colored melanosomes
  mosaic chirping on alder branch
Crunch of leaves   the only rubble
Pipelines run still   oil   only in stories of laughing elders
Rivers skip through land clear
Soil knows nothing of generational curses
Internal compasses of migrating birds search sky aligned to stars   hearts
  never misled by garish glow of shopping center signs
Only moon   illuminates paths for baby sea turtles to find ocean
Whale songs instead of noise pollution
Land is sovereign and every body is a sovereign land
No body is weathered
Forever chemicals stop being produced when all the children skip away from the mines
Cell phones all dead   never revived
Letters in drawers   in closets   under pillows
Blood circulates clear of all those things no one could ever pronounce
New science is understood as old truths
Turf is gone and stadiums burst with gardens
  No more NFL but at least every body knows nourishment
Lawns don't exist and six trampolines on one block is unthinkable
Neighbors are friends who know each other's kitchens
Children   wild outside and no one thinks to call CPS
    collections of little orchestras bouncing through streets
No standardized tests or worksheets at desks
Teaching and learning happen through play
All the guns melted into instruments
No such thing as a military game   only games
Billionaires only in history books
History books tell whole histories so tomorrows can be better
Prayers after every ending

WARNING

SUN   MERCURY   VENUS   PLUTO   ALL IN SCORPIO | THE ASTROLOGY STEREOTYPES ARE TRUE | WEDNESDAY ADDAMS IN FLORAL PRINTS | LITTLE MISS DOOM & GLOOM | EITHER DRUNK OFF WATCHING EVERYONE DANCE OR COLLECTING EYES WITH MOVEMENT | SISTER OF SILENCE | OBSERVANT | KNOWS HOW TO BE STILL | KILLS WITH AN UNREMORSEFUL TONGUE | BEAST OF FIRE & WRATH   what is this talk of water   but yes   there   whole oceans unnamed   what do orcas call a wave | TWISTS LANGUAGE INTO A BRAID | KEEPS PHONE ON AIRPLANE & HATES TEXTING | DOES NOT LAUGH AT WEAK JOKES | "That was a joke."   I KNOW | UNAFRAID OF AWKWARD | ZERO TOLERANCE FOR BULLSHIT | SEVERS TIES WITH A QUICKNESS | TRUSTS DREAMS MORE THAN WORDS OF MOST PEOPLE | COMES WITH SOMATIC PAIN IN RESPONSE TO STRESS | FORGETS TO EAT | OBSESSED WITH PERFECTION

like dew   so perfect
        on bare feet beneath a dark moon

Seeing

Five years old   first dream   first nightmare
Me   eyes quiet water outside my mother's door
I know she needs sleep

When she stirs I tidal wave
  into the room unable to explain my state   language
  for epiphany of death   absent

My mother is far away and I hear her voice
Cosmic connection   When we answer the phone
  each thinks to dial at the same moment

  but one of us dials first
  and the other says *I just picked up my phone to dial you!*
  and we laugh   or we sigh   depending on how air moves inside us

This is how our path unfolds
Those who come before us pray
  and it is so

When Death smiles at anyone in our line
  no one is ever surprised
It was seen

We all know why
  and still   we tremble crying
          limbs with barely any turgor

Histories

I ask my father
  about before I had my eyes
He tells me

  names   years   places
  bloodlines dispersed across borders in disguise
I ask my father

  about his youth   who he wanted to be
His voice paints a picture of a boy sailing skies
He tells me

  how he grew up to fly with Rangers
  how the military gave him a prize
I ask my father

  why shaking a president's hand
  can't offer ease to each aching sunrise
He tells me

  about sounds of want
I want to know so much
I ask my father
He cannot tell me

Orb: Do Not Disturb

> *Earlier, a tractor was used to cart dead pilot whales on to the dry sand, where researchers began taking blubber and teeth samples to try and understand why the mammals beached.*
> —The Guardian, July 26, 2023

Silence   My phone flashes but does not ring
I am my father's emergency contact
  watering the garden   voicemail full to the brim

When he tells me my name rests at the top of his list
  I do not ask who might redact
    joy from my day   if they will be someone who knows his grin in a silence

I tell my father I need to know what to do
  and think of pilot whales   how it seems they act
   against self-interest when

   bodies end enveloped in sand and air
My father signs a contract
  because dollars demand   he   you   I

  we   serve our purpose
Ignore songs in water   extract
  attack   reenact histories of bodies

  bloated with grief
Whales left on shore become abstract
  art   Who cleans fleshy red graffiti

left behind   Military orders and sound pollution
sever sonar songs   steal fathers   distract
with red white blue promises   bloated

information   Leave bloated oaths on poisoned lawns
We paint our bodies in wind   I do not refract
  grief   When my father calls   sand and air envelop each silence

Ways I am Like My Mother

We both see in dreams
  paths toward grief and Golden Fleece
  How the world of the living never redeems

Our lives   dramatic movies with all the same themes
  girls with mothers whose men disturb peace
We both see in dreams

  signs of looming cruel regimes
     and flashbacks to rough hands that still don't release
The world of the living never redeems

Our trust goes to the moon who beams
  in golden light and glows cerise
We both see in dreams

  how a bird can make reason burst seams
  and turn us to monsters worse than police
  (who the world of the living never redeems)

My mother and I hang wind chimes from our screams
  so we can be music through each stormy caprice
We both see in dreams
  how the world of the living never redeems

Kill the Messenger

Sickness binds us all to one place
I learn myself across mornings on my balcony
   between pesticides and highway-scented sky
An angry white bellbird dwells below   A pair of lovebirds live above
Details once like shy ghosts gather solid shape
   and etch new engravings in previous perception

It's all a matter of perception
   whether a bird is foreshadow or animal of a place
I am of my mother   Any avian shape
  bearing a message from balcony
  into home is a message from above
   a letter from worlds beyond sky

I let the cat become a hunter of the sky's
   jewels and show no remorse for fruits of my perception
It is known   birds who leave homes above
                         and find themselves flapping against ceilings are not of a place
                         where atoms have consequence   A busy balcony
                         unable to stop an intruder does not let in the shape

         of positive vibes   The incarnation of Hermes stills   shaped
by the cat into piles of quiet   Blood colors carpet apocalyptic sky
I drink wine after watching throat ripped from omen   Creatures hurtle through balcony
into apartment and my response makes the secular say my perception
is off   call my imagination too wild   They place
the tangible world higher than all else   above

every instance of genetic memory   Once   a bird came from above
and landed in our living room   Then   my brother shaped
into a form too fragile for this place

   craved to stretch beyond confines of a womb   sought sky
   in a way that altered our mother's perception
He flew out of her body and across the balcony

   into an unmarked grave we tried to find later   presumed success on a balcony
   overlooking unmarked remains   plans already in the works from above
   to take another loved one soon   to let another bird dispel any perception
   that flesh is merely flesh   When a room allows shape
   of feathers to fly in from outside   a soul leaves its body for the sky
Don't tell women in my family birds are just creatures of a place

Perception has doors   a balcony
   seats in a place we can each rest our heads while a bored God above
   watches   sighs   sends shapes wrapped in feathers to trouble us from the sky

YouTubes My Mom Sends Me

in middle school I had two cats

they were toddlers always attempting to
cross a glass bridge
and falling into a pool of water

anytime they tried to braid my hair
strands always ended up tangled

messes of curls
babies angry with mom
each time I laughed at wet fur

eventually they went where they were
 appreciated
with children allowed to let them inside

maybe they became a pride of
domesticated
descendants of saber toothed tigers

entering our home
feline and Fancy Feasts

maybe an animal services worker
made them past tense

maybe our strays ran for the mountains

now there is no one to call

now on this land
we have bears
or they have us

until the video
the police state is a channel
refusing to be deleted
no leaving behind america

proof doesn't mean people believe it

no goodbye

even living off-grid
in a shipping container home
Minneapolis will have its way
with lots of style

a tiny Texas town will have its way
this country will have its way
each time I see a man hit the floor

                              a piece of me dies
so many
so many men   unbelievable sightings
                              rounded up by the city
                              by the state
                              like cats

Doll

Go to the store.
Buy a few bags of cotton balls.
Pile them high in your arms and hold them close.
Take them home and mix them with jasmine petals
  so they are part flower. This will be their body.

Buy a new needle and thread.
The ones you have now will not do.
Materials to make your child
  must be unused or kept just for this time.

Look at the fabric.
Choose the softest material you find
  so their skin knows ease lingers close.
Make their clothes white. Sew on shells
  for eyes because their spirit is of water.
Mango core will beat as their heart.

They will have a cinnamon bark nose and full lips
  of hematite beads. Tiger's eye birthmark for protection.
Make them brown like a tamarind seed.

Go to the abandoned bedroom.
Find the box in the closet filled with
  treasures collected before your first kiss.
Pull out all the crushed, dark feathers
  you found in the street and at the park and
  while riding your bike. This will be their hair.
Make it wild. Make it a mess.

Dress them in jewelry of amethyst stones
  so they know to trust their spirit and
  see truly when they dream.
Add black tourmaline to ground them and keep them
at peace. Let their feet be bare so
  they are all the way of the earth.

When they are all sewn up and glued and kissed hard
  in those places they may fall apart, take them outside
  in the night. Let them bathe in the moon. Cover them
  in tears and give them some blood and praypraypray
  they become enough until later—

when they are let through to breathe and crawl and
run and cry and smile. Pray that while you follow
the rules, wait, exercise the most excruciating
patience, they take away the hole keeping you
awake. pray.

Sick Day

Period came to wake me
   announced its presence on yellow fabric two days early
     red Rorschach stain paintings of *The Cave*
                       Spooky Old Tree
                       Afraid of the Dark
                       every Berenstain Bears story written for Halloween

Do others see images in blood
Each time I open eyes   signs everywhere
Dear God show me something real before cotton soaks in sink

Before today there was yesterday   when I vomited twice
                             that first hope kneeling before porcelain
                             for false signs of life

The water turned the color of sunset
                        high AQI
                        unsafe
                        not fit for breathing
                        not habitable for life

Dallas, Before E

Moments drop like leaves in autumn
  so casual   so unnoticeable
  so plentiful
I laugh skipping through frivolous time
Dress lips in deep green   make body into a sensuous crime
  leave quiet home searching
  for ecstatic moans
  to drape cold bed in sweaty warmth
I revel in collecting want
Scorpion siren delighting in the sting
Deep down   never satisfied with the taking
  the tender flesh that always wants more than I have to give
I never invite bewilderment
My Mercury always clear   direct
I never forget my center
I can want part of a thing without needing the whole
Give me the hardness without the headache
Save feelings for someone with appetites for stress
I am surgical   no mess
It's not cruelty if conditions are spelled out at the start
I lose count of hearts eaten as midnight snacks
So many swipes right
So much same
Where is surprise
Where is the one who makes poets write
Where is the one who empties poets of words
I want someone with whom to share silence
No one shows me the stars
I want a hand to hold through sparkle of dark forests
Let us listen to owls and not fear death

Once   I took a workshop on bird language
Walked around my block searching for chirps
Ignored the nest I knew right outside my window
I arrived back home empty eyed and empty eared
How strange to not see a single flying being in such a vast sky
The only avian treasures were the feathers nearest

How many times were we in the same place
unaware   unready to hear each other's music

"Lost Valley is just a microcosm of the world."

When someone says they won't speak in the circle
  and they *no longer feel safe in this container*
  it is my face they see with closed eyes

Anarchists govern by consent
  and lament restrictions placed on touch
  enough   to tempt sickness

Our country is a scattered flock
  unstudied in the ways of *Sturnus vulgaris*
We see the art in the birds' flight   but not their connection

If we were starlings   we'd work together
  move as a murmuration   one breath
  to keep each neighbor from becoming prey

I am painted as Big Bad Wolf   *Canis lupus*
  howling too loudly for us to all beware
  the hunter armed with body aches

  a dry cough   stroke
His hold on weakened lungs
  or how he might aim his gun at an elder

  mean nothing to those with everything
Red hats   tie-dye shirts   competitive mimicry
  in which both groups of birds fail to flee the falcon

I keep ending up places
  where others refuse to creatively use and respond to change
Everything was bigger in Köppen climate Cfa

   trucks   stores   patriotism   southern hospitality
   for dinner   dessert   pecan pie topped with white supremacy
   (and record-breaking hurricanes)

Csb offers Douglas firs and so many
  ecstatic dancers blinded by oxytocin
  they haven't learned love requires action

I plead for mutualism   antipredator adaptation
  masks and social distancing   preparation
  in a time of unprecedented fires

We watch an army of coral snakes
  slowly slither closer
Those around me crown them kings

Duplex

after Jericho Brown

A man with a gun troubles the air
He sings while I sleep   He laughs where children play

At the store   where children play   where elders pray
Twice in one week we find ourselves grieving

Twice in one week we find ourselves grieving
First   eight people dead   Six days later   ten

First   thirty people dead   Six nights later   me
Dreams and waking nightmares compete for shrieks

Dreams and waking nightmares compete for points
Whichever wins the most tears gets a prize

The most dissociation gets a prize
Uvalde reminds us of Newtown which

 reminds us to know the exits in case
 a man with a gun troubles the air

Patterns

My uncle lives with many plants   Most he doesn't need to water
He says rain does its work   I guess age teaches patience
When *God saw that the wickedness of man was great in the Earth*
  and They sent down so much strain on lungs
  did They *smile*   Their *work to see*   Do They smirk now   repeated history
                         and broken promise?

God said They wouldn't curse the ground again   If God can break a promise
  we can't expect much of mortal men   Uncle Roe lives in Florida where water
  bleeds red tide   Algae blooms in my homeland make a new history
In Tampa   600 Tons of Dead Fish Washed Onto Beaches   My visit teaches patience
I returned to the gulf hoping to feel warm waves slither across skin   salt spray tease lungs
God had other plans   had to show displeasure on this patch of Earth

  while we were here   Where can we go on the Earth
               safe from Their wrath?   We cannot flee karma   Sometimes a promise
should be broken for the greater good   So many lungs
  across the world succumb to a plague not water
COVID stalks streets stealing more than firstborns while governments call for patience
  people do not know   Isn't that how we got in this mess anyway?   History

transforms like a restyled dress   These days   history
  classrooms implant alternative facts into young minds   hide ways Earth
  hurts from our lack of patience
  while <u>World Geography</u> and <u>American Promise</u>
  leave out how Atlantic water
  devoured Black bodies   lungs

  turned to vessels   Funny   how God scatters patterns   Look closely and lungs
mimic vessels of plants   branches of trees   walnuts and hemispheres of brain   History
  shows us scattered patterns we ignore   Water

swallows islands of the world while we play Russian roulette with the Earth
In some story   God made a promise
 said   *I will not again curse the ground any more for man's sake*   Do we have patience

made in Their image   or do we just procrastinate? Some say patience
 is a virtue   but how long must we wait for lungs
 to be safe? Some man made a promise
about change we can believe in   but he was still history
wearing no clothes in his parade   begging us for faith while Earth
  sighed and collected sludge across water

I promise myself to strive for deep adaptation   acceptance   patience
My uncle doesn't water his plants   His 83-year-old lungs
  don't complain about humidity   He's seen enough history to trust the Earth

Cohabitation

Human infants need touch to thrive
Naked eyes see sky as blue
These aspects of science are true
Genetic memory   an archive

  of ways it is possible to survive
  hot days / cold nights   If each neighbor of a different hue
            offered hands for review
    each pulse would sing of being alive

The virus eyes dancers
 who skip duets for a solo
  no harmony or beat
            just movement to music no one else hears

When I wake up a frightened doe   fleeing unknown threats
 he pulls me into safety of his heat

Project Yarrow

Coffee grounds make soil deep space
I mix them into powdery spell
  yarrow as the base

Names are not things I chase
I wait for flora to whisper   for songs   fragrant yells
Coffee grounds make soil deep space

Life everywhere beyond what eyes can place
I save grounds and blend them into spells
  yarrow as the base

Wound Healer   give me some grace
  through what weather foretells
Coffee grounds make soil deep space

  so my hands massage them into dirt with praise
I let peace blossom in my umbra like benign growth in a cell
  with yarrow as the base

We design a garden   lace
  each zone with goals and prayer bells
Coffee grounds make soil deep space
  yarrow as the base

Frequently Asked Question

after Camille Dungy

What are you having?

monsoon tucked behind a rainbow / seed / revolution / an end to all complacency / a messier home / medicine needed to grow / the change Sam said was gonna come / the change I wish to see in the world / less desire to scroll / an offering to my ancestors / a joining to them / battlecry & balm / future worth fighting for / the most dramatic movie / the best comedy show / photos too sacred for Facebook / questions without right or wrong answers / less sleep / a living dream

Of Naming And Not

I learned to listen by watching my mother sit still
She made me into a sieve
Skin pulls in particulate matter
Nana sends a breeze
  of Elizabeth Arden's Red Door in times of stress
When I find myself a wall   my grandfather's smile
  reminds me to be kind and turn the other cheek
I rarely succeed
I have trouble feeling worthy
  of hearing so much guidance
How often do ancestors shake weary heads
I leave the door open for God
Instead   he who offered hard fists knocks
  on my door with gifts of large animal tongues
I close the door in his face but
   the bracelet Gowri gave to ward off the evil eye still breaks
    its broken chain in grass buried by percussion of pulse

Names floated down through generations like old clothes
Before me   how many Mortimers and Anna Maries
  had no choice in how they called their children

Once   my mother woke to a glowing girl
She said I named myself   prescribed specific instructions
Teach me teach me teach me
                    everything you know

She teaches me to listen
Me and my man listen together
  waiting for our child to offer their name
We tell everyone to call them Baby

Every few days   I dream of them
Every few days I wake without hearing a name
Last night they came glowing   ravenous translucency
Me   fears my body could not provide
 but they latched to my right breast
Lifeforce flowed between us
Listening   connected   still no name
 still   having everything

"Lost Valley is just a microcosm of the world."

Call me riparian zone
I am home to so much no one can see
Mycelium networks form inside me
   cells ever-expanding into heartbeat brain bone
I relinquish any right to be alone
No more floating through days   free
   of tasks or worry   Each tree
    reaching toward sun is at risk of disease   drought   men who think they own

   what God made   & isn't that the constant joke?
Sacred meadow   brown skin   all enduring blazing fire
   without consent   so often told to focus on the rainbow
When we do give voice to all that broke
   open wounds of tomorrow   today generations prior
    fear is a scythe   vibrant futures not allowed to grow

"Lost Valley is just a microcosm of the world."

Fear is a scythe   vibrant futures not allowed to grow
   the world I want for my child
My mother made me wild
   enough to defy those who say go slow
   take time   Even as snow
   melts   and oceans rise to swallow cities   anyone asking for truth is reviled
   'Black Lives Matter' removed from sight so positive vibes are not defiled
When I speak to my mother on the phone   I do not show

   all the ways I am in pain   I tell her of nausea and aching breasts
   inability to leave bed before noon
I leave out how sleep breaks at the seams
   and days all offer tests
   scorched earth and unheard pleas   fragile hearts immune
   to dangers that came last night in my dreams

Orb: Dream of Earth

Water floods dreams while sweat becomes rivers
Body responds to soul   Slivers of age through cracks of sleep
Sometimes I wake up sobbing unable to remember why

War was all the talk until black robes stole the stage
Don't act so surprised   This story is as old as deep
space   Dystopian tomorrows take shape inside water

Filtering out forever chemicals costs too much
Not enough money to keep cancers away   Better to keep
people calm and instead send billions and bombs for war

Each dream   more vivid   Endings and beginnings
Ouroboros showing green after fire   Years ago   I saw my mother weep
in a dream of dire devastation   Back then   filtering

divinity's whispers was impossible
No need for cards when rest lets tomorrow's secrets creep
into today   I stopped praying before bed and upon waking   Each

step closer to God pulled me closer to others   It was too much
All the worlds I inhabit leap
into one cosmos   String theory evades me while physics tries to explain divinity's

will   Leah speaks of memory   experience   dreaming
                past   present   future   Sheep
awakened to their counting   For once   she is a step

nearer to sunshine   I have no hope so-called leaders will step up to the moment
I live divinity's vision each day   dig with a baby on my back   steep
tea reading news while war comes filtering through each day   I only dream of water

Orb: Forms of Worn Out

Offices Dangle Beehives and Garden Plots
  to Coax Workers Back
I can't tell if exhaustion stems from headlines or the baby

My doula says take breaks slow down
  limit reading news   Instead I snack
  on NYT articles reminding me of offices

where women tried to touch my hair How to enjoy harvesting honey
  or planting seeds when what the body wants is safety survival a lack
  of rising cases with changing leaves   My

timeline loads friends lamenting phone calls from ISDs
  about outbreaks of disease picket fence and cul-de-sac
                    american dream world where

no one is protected   What does it mean to birth a child
when men in suits demand they strap on backpack
and march into certain sickness   Each projected timeline

for when life will return to normal remains as unrealized
  as our desire for something better   I black
out my sky with sleep   cry and no one

witnesses grief how I laugh and bawl simultaneously
because capitalism uses nature to soundtrack
needless suffering and death And anyway what is normal for

witnesses of murder across screens without warning
Killers beg for votes   no timeline for futures sweet like lilac
Nina hums into chasm where my faith lived   Dreams of wilderness in place of offices

Of Rivers and Futures
for Ángel

This morning a friend said a water glint
  is science trying to explain kiss of wind & sunlight

This land   so much bloom & blossom while
  the city mows through dragonfly song

      Floral Farms / Shingle Mountain soil all lead
          Joppy / air a choking hand around necks

      In Sandbranch
      water doesn't flow from faucets

No government cares to report its crimes
They cut down forest defenders like they cut down forests

Every city is a cop city   every waterway an aspect of the divine
Akokisa River / Intrenchment Creek

We sit along the water & cicada song fills sky
A camera watches us watch all the wonder

 & what is left to do but shake our heads and sigh
 & what is left to do but throw our heads back & laugh

This too shall pass

Orb: Climate Collapse is Fucking up my Birth Plan

Uninvited guests line up at the door of future
   bringing blessings of plague   racism   fire
Plan C becomes Plan A   homebirth discarded for an unknown place where

                skies are not filtered in sepia
The entirety of Oregon is covered in drought and heat shatters all prior
   records   Our time with the ocean is uninvited

like us on Grand Ronde lands   Decades of logging and no controlled burns
                   make forests beg us to rewire
                 ways   I change the things I can and hope skies

bleed only clean air   The Serenity Prayer guides us to a coastal rental
                near hospitals where doctors don't admire
                slicing me like

sweet fruit   Half of medical students think it's true I feel less pain
          than someone white   My desire
to labor away from perceived expertise makes others bleed

disbelief   Our baby is due on my birthday
       just before contests for whose costume can inspire
 the most fear   The world wears masks for fun in sweet

   games of being gruesome   Once   scary movies only existed on screens
                   and air wasn't a choir
singing orange and pink murder ballads   I read news and don't remember disbelief

Games of cheating Earth somehow inspire disbelief
when sweet games of profit bleed like disaster   When skies require
 we read smoke like tea leaves   flee   This is what it means to be uninvited

Again Birthing Again Birthed Again Again Again

Prophecy
  same birthday
  Devil's Night due date
  a pair of waning crescents
  waterwater everywhere
Instead
She decides to be so much air
So many fives
October fifth at 2:05 AM
five pounds   five ounces
twenty-five days early

My neighbor walks in worlds beyond our eyes
The night my wate/r broke   so many
                        so many spirits at their bedside
                        so many

Our midwife says the baby's heartbeat is too fast to stay at home

                                      Those advising against our home birth don't
                                      know all the ways this country tries to kill us

I pack a framed image of my nana for the birthing room as if she isn't already there
                                            my loudest cheerleader
                                          waking up the neighbor
All proper nouns with faces that make up my face
                                 my rage   the way I purse my lips when shy
                                 hold me   keep fear away

I wish this faith was a constant but

my mother says *Hospitals are where we go to die*
By *we*   she means anyone not white

Texas likes to eat Black people round with futures
My body   home in Dallas   might have been swallowed
 by the highest Black maternal mortality rate in the country

I say *I want to feel everything* and the blue pill is peddled like something sweet / so many people want to obsolete intuition / tell me to lie down on my back and let the medical industrial complex go against gravity / *Just to be safe* / *Just in case* / Me with no energy to explain fear I feel at their vision / Everywhere everyone has questions / Everywhere everyone wants to tell me what to do
but

>   who dares tell Wind what to do with their body?

>   Sterile white walls steal me
>   and still

>   on my knees   inside myself   I see flame of her come through
>   My face stretches in ecstatic scream
>   I hold the stardust of her safe
>   The symmetry of my hips
>   e   x   p   a   n   d   s
>   Red and pink sunset flows
>   Earth of me ruptures open
>   I am held safe by her
>   We hold each other
>   My bones move
>   She is here
>   So new
>   My mother is right
>   I die   shedding old self
>   I am so new

Orb: Bloodletting

Blood is not something I'm afraid of
In highschool I was obsessed with the vampire
They were the most beautiful monsters before

  beauty standards evolved to offer more
I know what it means for a Black girl to admire
  pale skin   slender form   no part of her blood

  expressed phenotypically
Adulthood saw my acceptance for status quo expire
When my ex said I was too radical our marriage dissolved like artificial beauty

Alone   my mother's constant reminder: *You know   your eggs are drying up*
While so many in my generation saw circumstances too dire
  for procreation   I wrote poems of longing   expressed

  grief for a child who didn't exist without believing she'd come
Now   whether I want to or not   I must leave bed   drink water   respire
My daughter brings new reasons to live but also new reasons to fear   *Alone*

  is not a word I know anymore
Even in the tub I worry   inquire
  silently about her hunger while watching lochia paint red plumes of grief

  in water   My body mourns its emptying   I leak
  from between my legs and from my breasts   so anxious to let my baby acquire
  what she needs   Little vampire is

strong with bloodless latch   In her grip is no antidote to grief
Still   she alone the only monster not monstrous   Little crier
  surviving this love expressed as milk   her beauty a thing of my blood

Inheritance

Like light inside a plant   I exist beneath the baby's skin in ways no one can see
Forget the hair's curl or how her mouth unfurls in doppelganger smile
I am there in her anger
how she examines a face
with silent rage before the shriek   *Give me give me give me*
It is always time to feed her

People advise us to stick to schedules   give her
milk according to a clock   turn off lights at night so she can't see
They say babies should always sleep on their backs   She lies against me
tiny cheek pressed to a breast larger than her head   smile
through memories of the life she left to get here spreading across her face
and then the waking   the slow wiggle before the anger

There is no time to meditate or to do yoga or anything to shrink anger
when I open the *New York Times*   I pray for her
to be moved by the world's crimes through wrath toward healing   may she turn her
    face
toward someone who knows not what they do and see
the humanity beneath the fool   *Dear God please let my child smile
more from joy than from irony*   and I mean: Let her be more like her father and less like
    me

My mother cannot know all she gave me
how I cut myself from the world when anger
blossoms like a stapelia   stench of a hopeless smile
sensed across swaths of silence   My mother blames her
sadness on her children   the fact she doesn't see
us in the flesh   each face

she gave birth to visiting via screens   I face
the mirror with daughter in hand and try to remember the me
who existed before the mother   I stare at the glass and see
thinner hair and stronger curves   tight jaw   the low anger
my mother will never know I have because her
grandmothering is strangled by distance   On video calls   I smile

I focus on the bright bloom of carrion flower   balance out smile
from my mother as she buries her face
in succulent points   I aim the camera at the baby   offer her
some sunshine that at least she has this legacy   me
across the miles passing on the anger
she taught me to feel   I see

my daughter grow each day and her smile
becomes more and more like my mother's   I see the little face
look to me for comfort   I pray new worlds rise from her anger

Tornado Sirens When You Have A Sleeping Baby

a singing refrigerator / a baritone front door / the porch door / the metal songs of the cabinet door releasing scents of cinnamon coriander cloves

QAnon in school boards / judges robes / Congress

any and all doors ever made / the creaking wood of the floor / silverware on a plate / the fall of Roe v. Wade / the metal top scraping a glass jar of peanut butter / baby birds nesting outside the chimney / a sneeze / a neighbor mowing or blowing leaves / a neighbor parking / Juno barking / the taste of sepia smoke swallowing sky / the kitchen faucet / the toilet flushing / a mouse exploring the kitchen / some rodent reading in the walls / sudden jitterbug of a fly / a phone you thought was set to quiet / a phone falling off the bed / fingernails scratching your head / the fall of affirmative action / Proud Boys / Women Talking / truths behind horrifying fictions / horrifying truths

collections of collective griefs

the gasp during that first new episode of Black Mirror where **FATIMA** appears across the screen in Netflix Graphique / terms and conditions each time we sign / and haven't they been doing this since forever / make it look like a choice / contracts in unknown languages / listen to them tell us to recycle as if in that lies our redemption / Google *recycle plants near me* then find maps of race and wealth / this / everywhere / ours is the air they poison

Cop City / 61 protestors indicted for waging love / SB 63 come to stomp on mutual aid

your landlord bowling above in his living room / your shriek at reading news / silence about genocide from tiny town neighbors / this silence is a tornado siren / what is this world I give my daughter / what is this world / what is this world she wakes to each day / sirens everywhere

LET'S MAKE A MANGO ANTHOLOGY ALREADY

Hope Is A Sweet Evening Sky Ripening

I am Romeo sweet talking Juliet
She sways on balcony above
  blushing red

My arm extends toward her
  in adoration   tongue all compliments
  of beauty   all promises of love

You're almost ripe
I can't wait to eat you
Your juice is going to be so sweet

Adrift in green to sunset gradient
  I don't see the elder racing down his driveway
  Panama hat   highwater slacks

  island music of my grandfather
  in his voice   with none of the love
Gyal   yuh betta leave me mangoes!

His wooden cane waves as I flee
Words against my back about staying away
  but   my path to school does not change

I walk faster when traversing perfumed shade
Orange flesh never makes its way to my mouth
It takes gray hair playing in braids

  for me to hear broken language
    how I lay claim to the mango like Manifest Destiny
Hands never reach up to pull fruit from that tree until

  Earth Day   second grade
Me and my older cousin leave home
  with backpacks hiding empty trash bags

We don't tell our mothers the plan
  to pick up every stray piece of paper
  plastic   aluminum can

after school   First violence
          an unkindness of boys
             when we do not respond to courtship displays

Throats all threats spit through teeth
Loud flapping wings
Croaks turn to worse

  and they mob   One pushes my cousin
  and stands over her body sprawled on pavement
I become only anger

No claws   no impressive jaws
  no weapon or way to fight
  these boys beyond reach of words

  but   above   the mango tree
Unripe fruit becomes accomplice
I send a hard mango between shoulder blades

  of the boy brazen enough to start the roughness
Often   an unkindness of boys equates quiet with meek
This   is a mistake

My excellent throw lets my cousin get to her feet
A cacophony chases us the whole way home
  young patriarchal thunder persistent

  even after we make it inside our door
Feathers fly outside through peephole
  because boys want girls' gaze

  because boys want trash
  to remain on aching ground because boys put it there
Decades   centuries   millennia before

  and later   little is changed
Throats all threats spit through men's teeth   or worse
Generational curses dispensed by order of the state

  in the name of the law   according to men
  but through every unkindness
somewhere   sweet evening sky ripening

Anticipation

        my man reminds me again
about fruit softening on our counter
       he asks what circumstances
             would see me
              eat mango

when my body aches to be touched
it folds into itself at the slightest provocation

      the coffee is still in its jar
               kettle
             untouched

I have no space
for this question

this desire

          I let myself have it
      five days after its arrival

I want to make it a ritual
wait until
our home glistens quiet
alone   with only watching spiders

gratitude changes molecules in water
  plants kissed by soft sounds thrive
    music makes stomata smile wide
      capture more carbon dioxide
      more effective photosynthesis

let this experience have no interruption

pores open

not what the scientists boast about
#soulmateproblems

        this is a game of chess
               let flesh
   sleep when the baby sleeps
                   eat

king   queen   night
light candles   fill spices
play
give thanks

Abecedarian Mango

after Dan Vera

A is for *Anthracothorax mango*   Jamaican hummingbird   of least concern
Native resident of island sparking my grandfather's bones
Summers   third grade   me obviously from the States
My teacher only ever called me *America!* when spitting out my name
Now   I understand her distaste

B is for the boyfriend who renamed my cat Mango
  Both of them came seeking shelter   Van Gogh's eponymous feline
          made to sound more Black   more pops of color   more
          of places where different shades of vibrant radiate plentiful as stars

C is for convenience that lets me eat a mango in Oregon in December

D is for mango diplomacy   gift of fruit to prove goodwill between powers

E is for extinction eyeing Ethiopia   soil sparking my father's bones
  White mango scale takes its toll and fewer trees shade village gatherings

F is for frost-free like me   Give me heat
  Funny   considering I keep moving to where weather screams colder
  In Florida   rebellions after police robbed two lives from sunshine
                  the year I entered my mother

G is for green means not ready

H is for *The House on Mango Street* banned across my home state
  I see the face of my librarian at Bay Point Middle
          like flesh of my favorite fruit crumbling
          under fines and felonies

I is for indica   *Of India*
               like my grandfather's grandmother
             who took blue gods to Blue Mountains

J is for juice tributaries flowing through mangrove root arm hair
           falling into lakes at elbows

K is for Kalachandji's   where my daughter sips

   L   lassi like it will offer the ability to blow the biggest bubbles

M is for Mortimer   Grandpa who left Blue Mountains
               to sweat in Florida orange groves
   He only ever called me Pretty
       unaware blue-eyed girls at school unbraided his praise

N is for never have I ever let a mango go to waste

O is for only odes
   How many mango hate poems have you read?
   Some living beings taste too sweet to earn malice

P is for product of Mexico in Dallas
   Product of Mexico in British Columbia
   Product of Ecuador in the Willamette Valley

Q is for question   Who the fuck knows why some of us get mangoes in our lives
          and some of us don't?
            Maybe sometimes even God likes to be surprised

R is for ripe   meaning it folds into itself at the slightest provocation

S is for South Asia   across the world to   Florida 1833
                                        where   163 years later
                      me & my cousin get help from

  T Tommy Atkins   maybe Haden   some Good Samaritan
    who helped in our time of need on Earth Day   (second grade)
    by making hard body into weapon against boys

U is for urushiol knocking on roofs of mouths
  Unless allergies universal adoration
  How many mango hate poems have you read?
  Some living beings taste too sweet to earn malice

V is for violence
  of A   america sending bombs to aid a genocide
  of B   boyfriend who bruised my face like a fruit
  of C   convenience allowing me to savor a mango
   in Oregon in December

W is for words like bioregionalism rotting in snow
  while lustful mouth dresses sticky
  Outside   neighbors eat coconut purchased on sale
               all of us   embarrassed talking about sweetness
  We live in an ecovillage and should know better   but
  The world is burning anyway   right?
                         We're not the ones with private jets
  We bathe in deep adaptation
                  We wish each other warm fires on wood stoves

X is for XR   Extinction Rebellion
            the water protectors
               the warriors disrupting speeches made by suits who spit on peace
  I wish I was brave like angels swapping sweet juice for prison cells
     places where protesting is a crime

Y is for you only live once   carpe diem   take teeth to gutli
  Get to the center of everything   With everyone
                          I lose interest if tender flesh
                              flavor explosion

                    residue in need of cleaning
          never appear
          but who am I
                      to ask such intimacies of others?

Z is for zenith   time of power
                time of now   taste how sweet the yellow juice
                        how the seed of freedom scrapes against teeth

Poem About Pockets

Her face is The Sun as she successfully places a flower into her pocket
  all
    by
      herself
The Chariot carries her & I cannot sully the moment

It will be years before she knows
  this particular joy is usually only possible
  when we stroll aisles where blue dangles from hangers
The world is not designed to be easy
  for bodies not born male

 or
                or
              or or or or or
They give us pink pens and pink razors   but no pockets
I don't need pink on my razor   I just need it to be sharp

I don't need a razor   I just need to be sharp   Page of Swords
This world only wants us tender
                in acceptable ways   wants us to be delicate
                                          but to not believe in rest

What would Earth be if one part of the store didn't hoard all the pants with pockets / or if pockets were everywhere / if there were no divisions between blue and pink / if there were no divisions / if there were no stores / just joy / like children finding flowers / or discovering pockets / or the feeling of The Sun on a cool spring day

        when its warmth is the Most Gracious   the Most Merciful
        and not a God who gifts drought and wildfire

Prayers to Gentle Cat

My daughter stood at the top of some steps watching wind nudge leaves
A boy saw her adrift drinking in the beauty

He ran to her
He pushed her and ran some more   away

I could not move fast enough to get to her in time
She wobbled but did not fall

Aftershock tumbled across her face
Her turn of head to see a boy looking guilty

I asked the boy to please not push
I said *You could have really hurt her*

He was bigger   older   knew better
His mother made him say *Sorry*

My daughter stood for his apology and then took my hand
She led me to her room   I became her cocoon

She was not yet acquainted with cruelty
I call myself a poet but fail to find words for how men find fun

Sometimes I think about all the ways I cannot protect her
  how one day she will be doing something she loves   like watching leaves dance…

*

and I'm thinking about the choreographer killed for dancing to Beyoncé / I'm thinking about the Black man killed for being gay / I'm thinking about a piece of art named O'Shae and descriptions of his best friend's hands trying to keep him alive

*

Neela asks me to help her find rollie pollies
   and we dig until dirt gets moist
Everything needs water to live

  bugs and boys and little girls
  and everyone
  looking for pieces of wonder

Metallic sphere spends a whole sixty seconds
  in small palm before finally unfurling
My daughter rolls her wrist so the pill bug doesn't fall   giggles

  as fourteen tiny feet tickle her hand
She tries to protect the bug from harm
It's not so hard to be kind

Searching for Mary Oliver and Always Finding Men

The earth where fire burned last night
  still sends up tendrils of smoke
Today I will sit with my sisters who are not
  my sisters   We will look into each other's eyes
                  through a screen and speak
                  about our bodies being close again

Each of us built a new life
  away from Greg Abbott and Ted Cruz
We can flee Confederate flags but
  still end up where men seek domination

We write together & my lines are all seeds
  and soil about ways my daughter changes
  each turning of midnight   I cry
  and don't know if it's in gratitude for her body
  or in mourning for ways this world will try
  to shape it   I pray she has this quiet sunshine
                              clean air
                              agency to dare
                              be the truest version of herself
I read news and news and news and feel selfish
  for giving myself the joy of her wild and precious life

If people can have Huskies in apartments in Texas
  then surely   I can have this child
She smiles and does not know about rising heat or water
She smiles and does not know about men
  who send bombs to people her size
  flying kites   playing soccer   asleep in their beds

I don't know why I keep coming back to this world again and again

Maybe she is the reason
This summer day
Her smile

Indoctrination

after Miguel James

We have an unbirthday party when Neela turns six months / I make a joke that is not a joke about abolishing the police / My mother calls the next day afraid I disturbed the peace by saying too much

You can't just go around saying such things / There is a time and place for politics / You wouldn't want to offend your husband's family / You wouldn't want to offend a friend

I assure her I caused no consternation / No one who knows me could be mad / I ask why she isn't glad I honor her greatest advice / *You made me this way* / The years have made her nice

Sugar is dangerous in my family / My mother makes jokes that are not jokes about one day losing a leg / I pray my daughter won't inherit toxic traits / Instead / let her have the porcelain plates from Uncle Roe / I blame my mother for my every success / This includes strong opinions / This includes a big mouth

They say / you're supposed to let your children go their own way / Give them carrots and they'll still want cake / Play them Kendrick and they'll still want Drake / The truth is / I can't wait to indoctrinate my daughter

The truth is / it's already begun / At seven months she gained a distinct cry to be outside / Her tiny hands touch plants with wonder / We sing songs to the sky against the police loud enough to wake thunder / I want to pass on new tomorrows / When asked what she wants to be when she grows up / I want her to say happy and free

Ghazal for Abolition

The NAACP decides not to speak on abolition.
From Latin meaning *to destroy*. Their collaborators fear abolition.

My speech is removed from the schedule of events.
"This given setting and moment may not be right to cheer abolition."

For four years men managed the EPA without thinking of the weather.
Police sanction the March for Freedom but smear abolition.

It's the first day of summer, the longest day of the year.
I will spread ash across our garden and revere abolition.

Bonfires praise the season where burn bans don't exist.
We're fined for our Juneteenth fire. The climate weirds as I pray for a queer abolition.

Queer: *that which fundamentally transforms our state of being and the possibilities for life.**
We know one thousand beautiful ways to smash the status quo by engineering abolition.

Supermarket rainbows grace the chip aisle during Pride.
Under capitalism, nothing sacred. Influencers sell ads and commandeer abolition.

Think of prison reform, how Kim Kardashian became its surgeoned face.
Bangladeshi workers sew her slimming clothes in sweatshops. We need a more clear abolition.

I praise Neela when she colors outside the lines.
We use flower corpses to color the sky a persevering abolition.

An Astrology

1.

Once   in that place we go with no name on a map
   far from dirt path hugged by old firs and vine maples
      we both saw the stars move in the same choreography

Another time   through tent's thin fabric   I saw lights
   every shade of the rainbow dancing through trees
   across the water   and did not wake you

How glorious and eerie
   for the night to become *a coat of many colors*
   while we lie so far from the aurora borealis

Years later   we bring our daughter
We recreate a photo and now there are three bodies
   instead of two   We bring a friend and the four of us pray

   before breaking bread
When we reach the waterfalls   there are others
One is led by curiosity to gaze upon the face of our firstborn

   our daughter   who has your eyelashes and my lips and
   so much from ancestors whose smiles we do not know
Our baby turns away from the stranger twice

   and when the woman finally finds Neela's perfect nose   cheeks   eyebrows
      we hear _____
I think I must be in a Claudia Rankine: no:

Did I hear what I think I heard?
She sees my question   my denial of reality
   and touches our baby's feet while saying it again

Her fingers reach for your arm as her gaffe expands and you back away
My hand reaches out to be steadied
I shake my head as we create more space between us and loud opinions

When we stop walking   my eyes put the falls to shame
It's not long before we move off the trail to let her group pass

She sees my flash flood face and asks if she hurt my feelings
She says she thinks I'm beautiful   She says so much   I think it's great   really!
               My daughter is marrying a man from Congo!

And here I was   mad about a moment
   upset about climate collapse as we breathe in smoke
   but don't actually live near this fire

2.

To arrive at this patch of sacred
   we drive through charred trunks
Chimney gravestones mark where houses once stood

   beside a river named for its blue
When the Holiday Farm Fire swept through the east
   we fled to the west to find clean air

One day I woke before the whole world
   and found myself alone in the Pacific Ocean
Like a child   I rolled down dunes that lined beach

screaming joy into blistering sand

3

Sometimes I try to be different / *Dear God* / *Make me more like Joseph* / so forgiving of his brothers / When I walked away / when I walked away / when I walked away / away / away from the woman who touched the body birthed from my body / flesh of my flesh / it was because I was broken / Each step across moss was a prayer for me to be more like soft soil beneath us instead of roaring water ahead / When the woman found me again / half my tears were from shame: why was I not a dragon hearing *Dracarys*? / I wanted to see her burned / but when I opened my mouth words came out instead of flames / Her eyes found their own water even though I was gentle / even though I left out the way whiteness claims entitlement / how she behaved like everything the light touches is her toy / how she came so close in times of plague / and how / and how / and how I hated myself for not letting my tongue loose a tsunami / I thanked her for her apology and am not proud of it / *I will go down into the grave mourning* / My daughter entered the world without a name / It took six weeks of her eyes singing for us to hear *Neela* while rocking her at night / Baby who I promised to protect / When she waves to the hills / holly tree / stellar jay / rain beyond our porch upon waking / I don't know how I can ever be so consumed by rage / But then / each time she smiles / I feel the knife of me sharpening / more / and more / and more ready to draw blood

They say I'm a beast.

Men like to make fire
Since autumn brought rain to the valley   flames
   take longer to turn from whisper to choir

I like to watch my man aspire
   to see joy dance across his face of accomplished aims
Men like to make fire

   and gaze at light they bring forth with desire
   no fast or meditation or prayer tames
Take longer to turn from whisper to choir

   says my man when ire
      makes me destructive   hot   too impatient to play civility games
Men like to make fire

   and sometimes it's good   Charcoal is a purifier
My potential energy shames
So many tense necks because I go from whisper to choir

My body responds to stress in new ways   I require
   the sky hear me call God by all their names
My man learned to make a slow fire
I struggle holding rage   its whisper a perfect choir

Eye Gazing with Monsters

The day we planned our future
   snow layered porch
   trees   everything we could and could not see for miles
Whatever had been brought alive
   by our hands now waited for a funeral
We pray when we plant seeds

We sing goodbye when seeds
   do not see sky   Sometimes teases of green poke through to threaten future
   but pass before reaching full sestina   I plan a funeral
   for each plant and poem that dies on our porch
I gaze into eyes of a woman sprouting snakes coming alive
Beyond our driveway death floats through air for miles

My mother calls and she is miles and miles and miles
   away   My husband and I plant seeds
   she may never see grow   Our midwife helps our ancestors' dream stay alive
   but only for so long   Snow falls with no regard for future
I count bodies made stone stiff while centuries pass on our porch
I lose count of children killed by police or pandemic without funeral

Neither I nor my mother want a funeral
When snow blankets roads for miles
   mangoes of our DNA keep us on the porch
Our sighs spread beyond what can be traveled wearing bodies   Seeds
   I plant now will not know future
   for long   I laugh in disbelief at the possibility of a piece of myself being alive

   tomorrow   We quarantine so a seed now growing toward blue sky stays alive
Call me contradiction   I would not survive my daughter's funeral

Me and my husband plan our future

So many spreadsheets map unseen miles

I pray and laugh and cry simultaneously at the thought of seeds
   frozen by the gaze of the monster on our porch

A bathtub collects rust just beyond the graveyard of our porch

I climb in and the shock of cold against skin makes me more alive

I feel most colored against the sharp white background of toxic seeds
   america wants to plant   I tuck myself away to avoid missing my own funeral

Another name for future is Medusa   once beautiful   now monster who wants none of
   us alive

Elliot snaps a photo of my nakedness taking up miles

 and I post it online so I might exist into another future

We still plan what seeds to sow on our porch in the spring

I wear a suit made of seafoam to bury the world we knew   My smile is heard for miles

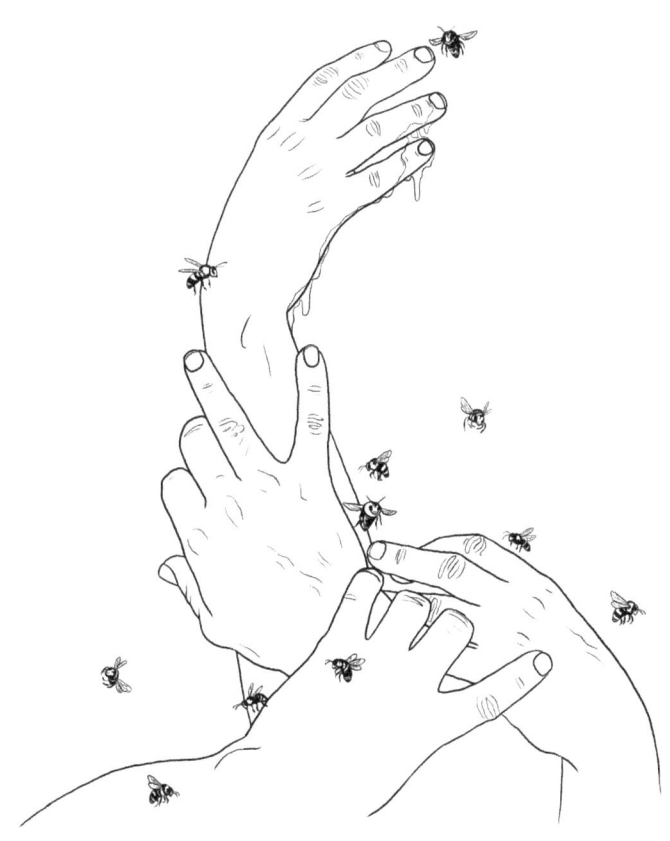

A Cautionary Tale

At night I become a sentry on a watchtower
    searching for peace instead of war

In place of asphalt I imagine blackland prairie
    purple coneflower   cedar sage

Come to Cabell Drive   I wish and envision
    four legs trotting down middle of street

Weeks since one visited me
    in dreams   Perhaps I learned whatever

    lesson the universe tried to teach
So much sleep in their company

So many encounters awake
A chase on my bike

  fear   a thousand bells ringing under my skin
        as I gazed into her eyes beside me   always   only ever beside me

Later   half a mile ahead   after
  she was scared away by a man louder

than my gaudy screams   someone offered a warning
Be careful   *a coyote is moving her pups*

    across the trail   It all made sense
Who could blame a mother for trying to keep children safe

Ask the Earth what she does to those who forget
    she is a mother   first

Hubris

O the glory of a seed

  That a tiny thing can stretch through soil and reach up to greet sky

Divinity in action
Do not speak of accidents

Do not suggest something so miraculous as an evergreen cone is happenstance

What is the Fibonacci sequence but God singing
   leaves   nautilus shells
                                                          all octaves of Earth

And us   just rats
        presuming to know the reason for the maze

Dallas, TX 2019 / Bishop Arts Typewriter Poem for Jim about Physics

All things in the universe want to be beside each other
Like gravity
        the set of eyes at the party we cannot ignore
Its magnetism beckons us to the floor and it shows us how to move
We show it how to curve   how to be law
                of existence on Earth
     how to become a flock of birds
                trying to paint a picture
                with weight of mortal bodies
And us   just starlings
        tinytiny things pulled through air
        by   w i n d
        made when God whispers

Victoria, B.C. 2023 / Government Street Typewriter Poem For Della About Turtles

So few summers to know the truth of the world
$\qquad\qquad\qquad$ Good things cannot be rushed

Think of turtles
$\qquad$ how they go   s   l   o   w
$\qquad$ how they don't try to bend time

The world spinsspinsspins
  while they barely bat an eyelash
Talk to them about the speed limit
  and they will ask about the last time
  you stopped to look at the sky

Don't be surprised
  at the wonders that find you
  when you move at their pace
The world contains more magick
  when we stop to take in awe

See   how they live so long
$\qquad$ still remaining tender beneath patterned shells

Tell a person to have such grace under boulders of time

August. Blackberries Everywhere.

Someone will call themself
in a hurry   notice a cluster
as they walk   dip off of the
road and extend an arm to
reach treasure guarded by
   thorns   The pause
after it enters their mouth
the closed eyes the smile
   the way they forgot
        time

Church at Prairie Fest

Once   God dressed me in finery
put me alone with no hand to hold
dancing   in a swarm of bees

Bodies dropped to the ground
Fear   the biggest thief
Me   the only tall blade of grass
        still swaying in wind
                radiating invitation
                for Queen and court
                to my inflorescence

                                                              One version of feeling most alive
                                                                 is 30,000 buzzing blessings
                                                                            across skin

                                                                                 I surrender
                                                               They are a body of water

                                                          I give myself to current
                             Spellbound   no thoughts   so lost

in holy music / so found in holy music
                drums and guitar fade / Brave Combo evaporates
                Cosmic hummmmm makes me phoenix into a deeper astrology

This   no stadium experience
I feel safer with the bees than in hives of people
None of these winged trumpeters will pull out metal

  and steal interstellar treasure

  from grieving galaxies
I cannot be in a mass of my own species and be present

Always / I know the quickest way
to the exit / to my car
  My husband's number taped to my driver's license

 in case some tragedy befalls me
In this field   those concerns become ghosts
I only feel blessings of bees

 and then   their strident absence
 a taste of what's to come   slow trophic cascade
                        so much quiet

God Silence

Limestone cannot teach me to tread softly enough across its skin
The cedar said my hummmmmming woke all the wolf spiders
How do I worship without disturbing preachers asleep in branches
   cawcawcalling me out for my volume
       My body is a poltergeist searching a kitchen
       My body weighs more than all the plastic in the oceans
       My body seeksseeksseeks like the copperhead   somewhere safe to rest
How free it must feel to be shapeless   unburdened by flesh
One day I will know how to absorb the sky's sermon
One day I will be quietquiet

Epithalamium

after Li-Young Lee

Wedding day   improvised vows beneath
  a tree three centuries old   Grandma Maple grows
  now without us   grants shade to the patch of earth
                            where we conceived our first child   We thought
those leaves would be a blanket to catch her birth
but God had sweeter plans than Lost Valley

I didn't consult my cards before moving to the Willamette Valley
I didn't ask what lived beneath
  shine or shadow of the man who initiated my new birth
I am the moon in your gravitational pull   Epiphany grows
  inside me and radiates outward   I only thought
I knew what it meant to love   Our history transcends Earth

I loved you before I was born. It makes no sense, I know. Earth
  and their Great Basin Bristlecone pine   their mountains   each valley
  is an infant beside our past   You were at the end of every thought
ever making its home in my body   Beneath
  before   between hours of each millennia   finding you grows
easier   This time   I first touched your face before midlife   Neela's birth

came early enough to open space for others   I feared my womb would never birth
new futures   I lost gleam pining for motherhood across cement-covered earth
When we want something long enough   desire becomes a ghost   Acceptance grows
like a nighttime fog flooding a valley
You were warm air   Destroyer of mist   We kissed in my car beneath
                            a streetlight and I thought

This is how Eve felt after eating that fruit   When you said *I want everything you want* I thought
there were limits   Women aren't taught to believe men   We birth

boys who learn shrapnel smiles   You break patterns   You are soft moss beneath
rock   I give thanks to every woman before me who left you clinging to earth
for me to find   Your father tells you to wait a year before starting a garden in my valley
  and we listen   I tell any flower lining my path how music between us grows

 and they roll eyes from lack of faith   Our harvest grows
  so bountiful that loved ones brew stories of glyphosate   Unreal   the thought
such green grass could cover a valley
I reassure my mother nothing changed after giving birth
I leave out details   how you touch me daily like a sailor who kisses sandy earth
Just beyond our porch   a cherry tree rubies view beneath

sky atop valley   I can't describe how sweetness grows
from so many leaves   Beneath above inside night   owls hear each thought
  and offer endings after birth   but my love   we cannot be contained by Earth

Time Simulation

I wonder how many times I have known you
  how many times beams of light left my body
    and found the equivalent of your center

One time   when we met we had no words   Another time   no mouths
Time proves the redundancy of bodies
Time says   *Skin is so limiting*   and I nod

We spend time playing hide-and-seek across universes and you
  sly smile   allow new fingerprints to saunter across my path
Accept my reverent tongue to arch   loop   whorl

I collect your perfectly chiseled jaws in my basket of planetary wonders
Today   you have a beard and a hardness   but
 I remember a time of soft and curve

Each taste of you leaves me incredulous with wonder
  that I could so please the AI in the sky
    building worlds on algorithmic fates

Scientists say there's a fifty percent chance
  we live in cascading green code
  and if that's the case   please

send my thanks to The Architect
    for surely   I have won the game
Surely   I have the highest score of all time

Generational Joy

I mentioned a craving for onion rings
  and days later your hands drip with batter
I didn't know a casual mention
  would get me such delicacies   at home

This is how our path would unfold
I say what I want and you say
 I want everything you want
 and it is so

We moved to the Blue Barn wanting roots
We arrived and grass turned to hay while acorns
  fell like cannonballs   (not the artillery
                    more like children

                  folded gleefully into spheres
                  who launch into wind
                  seeking water)
Land whispered to us across moonlit nights

 about what it could hold
 where the kale could grow
 how our baby would know names of
 so many more-than-human kin

Now   we harvest alliums in a new heat
Instead of rings you make pakoras from onions
  we watered together from seed
I dreamed of this life

 in the way a child dreams of being a ballerina

                        an astronaut
                        an athlete
                        Let me give myself to the Earth

And it is so
Each thorn we pull from flesh is a lesson
Greet the worms and be nourished in return
Plant red clover to steep soil in joy

 so generations of verdure afterward feel loved
Set baby redwoods where they can witness
  all the ways the valley changes across the years
Dance with each orchestra of bees

Leave windows naked
  so when our daughter wakes she is greeted by sky and breeze
Neela gathers sun alongside many seedlings
She walks clutching stalks of onion flowers

DREAM FOR EARTH

I pull a card surrounded by stained glass
The woman passing   passing   passing my avoidant pew
  is continuous hummmmmm of cars through splendor of trees   until

on knees   we go different ways to pray to the same God
I raise The High Priestess above my head
  and Tarot obscures my view of the man some say

tried to save us   I stay awake until 5:30AM watching videos
  of land where he was born   sob with others
into Instagram stories making us helianthus   hḗlios   sun

We become one all-seeing witness
Petals trade red hearts over sadnesses but
  what of our tears besides what our eyes have seen

Bodies of human children burned into unrecognizable beings
Sounds come out of places where faces once existed
  in hues only heard in horror movies

But   this is not a movie
This is not a drill in preparation for something worse
This is the worstworstworst thing

This is the story of yesterday
  and yesterday and yesterday
  trying to make us believe corrupt tomorrows

  sing songs we should move to
I watch a Dabke circle dance dare gunfire during
  the Great March of Return in 2018   I study maps from 1946

Operators of rude machines poison green eras growing
  dam/n rivers flowing in ways misaligned with greed
  think nothing of salmon or people cut off from unfurling

  future generations in ancestral homes
In Gaza   fifty thousand people rise each morning
  with full moon wombs   180 new babies a day

while tax dollars aid
  white phosphorus licking tiny bones
No   taxation without representation

Yesterday was the time to become ungovernable
Throw tea into harbor
Burn all the ships

Let us be sharper thorns
There is no great leader coming
They were all murdered by people who don't like flowers

When live oaks receive a storm   no single tree faces winds alone
Let us link together at roots
It is time to use teeth to protect one another

I feast on tender proselytizers of connection
  Naomi Shihab Nye and Ross Gay
  Jane Hirshfield and Mary Oliver and

  Aracelis Girmay and Aiyana's poems
  with their moments of shimmer
I write down gratitudes when I wake up   meditate

  try to dress every piece of wheat bread
  in flamboyant finery to balance out grief   and still
  in sleep   only nightmares trill in my ear

Wrens and warblers banquet on sunflowers we sowed in May
In October   cavalier   the man who calls himself owning land
  where we live wants to rid of what remains

I cannot stress enough how much life each Autumn Beauty gives to the ecosystem
  how they are so much hymn against gray skies
                              I am done trying to convince men what is right
Online   we smile into selfies and
  disguise words with numbers for pleas to be seen
FR33 P4lest1n3

Please   we just want everyone to be seen as human
                    Please   please   please
                    Let us stop saying please

              One way love can manifest is wrath
        To be a mother is to be tied to more than who came out of you
I fall to knees to kiss feet of every child whose limp limbs

  enter our kitchen through my phone
Glowing screen becomes comet across dark bedroom
I hope my moans wake our landlord upstairs

  who asks us to rid of flowers
Even after we are gone   they will return and return again
Soil does as much as possible to nourish through every threat

Earth hears every invocation and tucks them between water and wet rock
At the boardwalk   before a single written word   a prayer
Body bent over wooden rail   hands open

Sooke Basin   Strait of Juan de Fuca   Salish Sea   Pacific Ocean
May I open portals in others   Please lend me your strength
Make my language as powerful as your waves

I wonder if God hates hearing the word Please
  as much as I detest seeing it offered to oppressors
I let sidewalk chalk scream

Some woman walks by
   finds fault with even this meekness   says
 Some people might call what you're doing defacing

says   writing END GENOCIDE in ephemeral pink *is not the way*
On knees   without a prayer   hard fists gathered on thighs
  shaking in the place where disbelief meets lack of surprise

  all I can do to not break
   her   is to listen
She is all directives   No invitation for outside perspectives

I should have asked what to do
  when calls to Congress and voting fail
Tell me the appropriate response

  when legions of us are clenched jaws and forefingers
picking skin of thumbs   I pay for groceries inside a store
  and find myself transported across the street

  with no memory of moving feet
I lose count of moments
  my daughter looks at me afraid

  because laughter rolls where it does not belong
Ten silent days of ten-hour introspections   and still
  this attachment   to hope   this aversion   to what is

I wish I could say I wish my enemies
  only a change of heart
    but what I wish for are their hearts

In our thousands   In our millions
We will have what is due
May our thriving be retribution to all those who stand in its way

Black & White Scream

My hair is ungrateful for my love
Tincture of rosemary   biotin through teeth
  shampoo and conditioner free of synthetics
  and animal torture   and still   my care will never be enough
Thinning strands call no bluff
This is a definitive leaving   history repeating itself with no variation
In mirrors I see my nana   my grandmother   my mother   me
Four generations of alopecia
I brush my daughter's hair and wonder if hers will someday follow suit
  and run through options each time I sweep tumbleweed curls from hardwood floor
                                                    A purple bob wig for flamboyance
                                    Long seafoam waves so I can be a mermaid   play pretend
                                                Maybe I'll shave it all off and go full Wakanada
                                                          ask Jack to design a banyan tattoo
                                                              from top of head to roots

Probably   not much will change
I will walk into bright days with head covered
  in keffiyeh   a scream entering every quiet room

Solidarity

Wind and water know nothing of borders
A cut on your brow is a cut on my brow
We bleed together
Our griefs intertwine across time and distance
I don't know your name but I feel your eyes
I want to wrap my arms around your shaking body
I   too   am holding up the cold shell of who you love
I love them too
I love you like I love the ocean
The ocean does not know my name but feels my heart
Names can be so colonial anyway
Fuck Linnaeus
Did he ever write about knowing the souls of beings
My soul and your soul share the same cosmic thread
Stardust of your eyelashes forms cartilage of my ear
I try to imagine your laugnhter
People near me don't understand my tears
You are near me
I hold your hand through cancerous cobalt and bone-licking bomb
I try to find us a beach where waves are clear and clean
The breeze threads us together
This is telepathy
We are mycelium spores forming rain clouds
We are roots of trees talking beneath soil in ways no human can see
When you sigh I stir from my sleep
My love for you is a violence
My tenderness turns me into nightmare
I want to haunt all those who dare unbraid your glory
Any who cut our brows should be afraid

"This is the soul of my soul"

Spoken by Khaled Nabhan as he cradled the body of his three-year-old granddaughter, Reem, killed in an Israeli airstrike on Gaza in November, 2023.

I loved her / too / I love them / all / Always will / A new violence blossoms inside my bosom / I sing onyx into its sharpness / Surely / this is what the ones who did this / are doing this / want / right? / I want to give them what they want / What they want is not laughter on playgrounds / I want to be the thing they love / which is not peace / Inside me / a _____ aches / I cannot type words I want for fear of being dragged away / Politicians don't understand metaphor / This is a poem / This poem is not a threat / It is larger / Cradle this as promise / Our rage will bore into the next lives of those responsible / _____ on all their futures / Every time they fall in love their hearts will break / Every mourning tear we cry will haunt them past their graves / Each time they return to earth it will be to feel the pain they caused / There is no redemption / There is no apology for this / Damn these fingernails of mine / Damn these nostrils / Were I a god / I would be the kind to be feared /

but / I am only a mother

In An Emergency Room Watching Videos Of Gaza

Who is your family doctor?
Sometimes an absence has no name and sometimes it has thousands
This morning I drew The Tower and did not know I'd be here
A stranger says they've been waiting six hours
Across hours I lose count of dust-covered once-buildings

We watch 427 days of terrorism by the world's most powerful countries
Unlock phones   swipe
  through screenshots showing shadowbanning
  and friends with silenced accounts

How to not break at sight of toddler shivering from shock or cold or both
  black eye   red spot in center of right hand not stigmata
Another boy offers comfort through forever trauma
   with a face streaked in what Halloween face paint mocks

The UN gives children food-shaped toys
Worst ironies   Idiocracies   BidenHarrisMuskZuck want us to not look up and
  question why *Time* names Taylor Swift 2023 Person of the Year
  while journalists share their own eulogies

When their stories stop coming
   one by one   we are expected to celebrate
   the birth of a redeemer who clearly did not save us
Ceasefires just long enough for sales and shopping
   while the US House declares anti-Zionism is antisemitism
So many threats of losing jobs for decrying men stripped and kidnapped
   in front of sisters   mothers   wives
      brothers   neighbors   the world's eyes

Letters fall from a deceptive sky demanding people move south   south   south

   the place they called home divided into blocks with numbers
Everywhere guaranteed to be safe now   ashes   ashes   ashes
                                                     all fallen down

Again   again   again   me and my sister scream together over FaceTime
She tells me about being the honored guest speaker
   in a room with five cadets   each uniform a perfectly pressed menace
She didn't know they'd be there   went to where wails live
     opened herself and shared wounds without speaking proper nouns
A student waited for everyone else to leave and
   said *Thank you* for being louder than empire

I unlock my phone   drag thumb across screen
Across from me   a woman my age rests her head on her mother's shoulder
Meme   meme   meme
A baby a few seats away cries
Inside phone and nightmares
   580 IVF injections for a miracle to be stolen

I cry and someone thinks it's because of the plastic band on my wrist
398 minutes to understand why a knife inside my abdomen kisses me awake
A woman shrieks from behind sliding glass doors
NO ENTRY UNLESS ACCOMPANIED BY STAFF
I cannot see what's happening on the other side

In Gaza   NO ENTRY of food   water   aid
                                     but we all see what happens on the other side

In Canada   taxes are high   but I won't pay a dime for this ER trip
A woman grades papers beside me
Capitalism's clock refuses to stop
That's how we got here   right?
                        The dollars   billions
                        in natural gas and oil
                        in the land of olive trees

Systems that only see brown soil and brown people as fruit to be juiced
                    When sliced open   watermelons reveal colors of the Palestinian flag
                          In 1967 the flag was banned by israel for twenty-seven years
                                        I unlock my phone and swipe

Thousands of women holding bodies the size of my daughter
My period comes and I leak unprepared   soil favorite dress

It's 10 PM and my husband sends a video of our daughter reading to a friend
I see Sana Al-Farra in her Disney princess dresses
  and vow my daughter will never see movie funding death
I try not to let her see me swipe
 but she still senses the emergencies
   how they gather and multiply each day

March 2024

My father calls from Istanbul to tell me
 he's on his way to Djibouti

There   he will wait
                 for a summoning to Somalia

Most of my life   people asked
_____?

                never satisfied with my answer:
                456 stories woven from tongue split by fog

            thorns formed by travels of a wave
Thorns color of my mother's lipstick

 each time she spontaneously cut her hair
I always begged her not to do it   I never understood   until I did

This is a story of blast rock
When I grew up & took scissors to a mirror that first time   I recorded it

 advertised my brokenness to Facebook
 fashioned myself into David Attenborough

 describing some animal behaving strangely
 & isn't that the story of every polished headline?

But then   *$102,000 Raised for Man*
 Who Donated His Enslavement Earnings to Gaza Relief Efforts

& isn't this how we survive: all of us who have been stolen from
                         giving goodness to someone else?

Of course   newspapers don't say he's enslaved
They latch seventeen dollars & seventy-four cents

for 136 hours of work
to   words like *inmate   prison labor*

This is what happens
  when data comes second-hand

Before I knew the words
 genocide   empire   refugee

 I took a coin purse full of questions to my father
He filled it with dew

 that flew away from broken zipper
I can tell you how to mend a hole in a garment

 but not how to trap air   I failed physics
 & somehow made it through high school

I failed stats four times in college
  & never got a degree

I guess this is why I'm a poet
Don't give me formulas

I have always been tired of counting   but here I am
  keeping track of how many faces of grieving parents

 I can hold in my memory

Today   December 1, 2024

Over two hundred thousand Palestinians murdered
  with my tax dollars

Maybe I have a blood clot in my leg
Maybe it's the flour massacre lodging into my body

Ebo Taylor makes promises about Victory
  but I can't help but be bitter

Angela Davis says Freedom is a Constant Struggle
  but I am a toddler   who wants everything now

Planting Seeds

> *"And they are lucky that what black people are looking for is equality and not revenge."* —Kimberly Latrice Jones

Pregnant again   everyone tells me not to read the news   again
                                                                                                          so I watch
   not CNN or MSNBC or videos from the New York War Crimes
My device is a portal to genocide

Corpses fall away   replaced by rows
            of kale   beets   garlic scapes
A catalog of atrocities plays inside my head
  while my daughter asks to be pushed higher on the swing

She laughs suspended beneath regal cedars
  while I stand behind   hands pushing plastic seat
  our view of the garden a peace
  while I contemplate visions of vengeance

I see whites of the eyes of Kimberly Latrice Jones
  speaking about Black people
I wish every white person in the world could see her rage
                                                                our rage   our grace

A gathering of ravens is called an unkindness
A gathering of colonized peoples is called a fury
My genetic memory gathers skulls
My daughter kisses my belly and says *I love you*

I'm a big sister! she says
She is a star sparkling
I am a mother watching death

peck at children   How I dread Broomhill Park
Village Foods   endless improv to make my mood more tolerable

                                                I want to slice open the soft palm of my hand
                                  and caress faces of each acquaintance who asks how I'm doing

Remarks by President Biden on Recent Events on College Campuses / his truth in his lies

morning.

I **want**
 our

American

(Coughs.)

authoritarian nation **The**
American **tradition**

must
prevail.

our history

violent
the law

Vandalism, trespassing, breaking windows, shutting down campuses, forcing the cancellation of classes and graduations — none of this is a peaceful protest.

Threatening people, intimidating people, instilling fear in people is not peaceful protest. It's **against** the law.

Dissent is essential to democracy. But **dissent** must never lead to disorder or to denying the rights of others so students can finish the semester and their college education.

Look, it's basically a matter of **fairness. It's** a matter of what's **right.**
to cause chaos.

People have the right to get an education, **the right** to get a degree, the right **to** walk across the campus safely without **fear** of being attacked.

But **let's be clear** about this as well. There should be no place on any campus**, no** place in **America** for antisemitism or threats of violence against Jewish students. There is no place **for** hate speech or violence of any kind, whether it's antisemitism, Islamophobia, or discrimination against **Arab Americans or Palestinian Americans.**

It's simply wrong. There is no place for racism in America. It's all wrong. It's **un-American.**

I understand **people** have strong feelings and deep convictions. **In America**, we respect the right and protect the right for them to express that. But it doesn't mean anything goes. It **need**s to be done without **violence,** without **destruction,** without **hate,** and within **the law.**

You know, make no mistake: **As President,** I will always defend free speech. And **I** will always be just as strong in **stand**ing up **for** the rule of law.

That's my responsibility to you, the **America**n people, **and** my obliga**AIPAC**e Constitution.

Thank you very much.

Girl, Bye (These Boots Are Made For Walking)

When you said *I'm speaking*
  toothpaste from earlier protested
  by letting halitosis retake their House

Shadow scrambled from teeth   heart   history
  Madam Auntie   Progressive Prosecutor   Top Cop
    Boss Girl   Bad Bitch   Proud Daughter of Immigrants

  with no regard for children across an ocean
My grandfather came from the same Caribbean island
  as your father   grandmothers before & before & before him

  laughed jeweled draped in sarees
  like spirits still singing in your DNA
They say all skinfolk ain't kinfolk

  & your smile is what I see beside every brown hand
  raised to veto a ceasefire
Meme Queen's broken record mouth opens   scratches   spouts

  lies about working around the clock to make violence stop
  beside tired refrain *israel has the right to defend itself*
Three strikes only applies to people you locked up who look like us

Otherwise   red lines are made for crossing
  & war/crimes are fine if committed by allies funding campaigns
The internet accuses you of textbook abuser logic

  & I remember the ex who hit me
    how he asked me to choose
    between him & nowhere else to go
When I left him   it was so easy

Tell The Children

Herons talk about temperance & I laugh / In Dallas / my mother shakes her head / I dress the villain of myself in red & let my daughter play in my ribbons / On Ella Beach / I take her hand / We throw rocks / talk about ownership / untangle myths / listen to wind / It is possible to feel without singing coal / Am I broken if I dream of ruined suits & wake up smiling / Do my neighbors not wish for their children to know rage / I don't know what it is to love without wrath / Yes / let our children know tenderness / Let them hold & behold & be held by flowers / & too / let them know how to crush petals into a poison

Fecundity

When a single Israeli bomb fell
  on Gaza's largest fertility clinic

  it extinguished more than four thousand IVF sparks of life
Futures stopped blossoming

Universities   museums
  holy places holding histories   all ashes

The past is a ghost who never transitions
All of us   haunted

Spirits whose footsteps walk on hardwood take new shapes
They ask us to stop trying to sleep

  leave our room and go speak to the poltergeists
    confront the demons

I want to write a spell to banish genocide
  but the moon dies each night in plumes of smoke

My mouth waters prayers for a child
  & when my blood doesn't come

  I draw The Sun and Five of Cups
How many juxtapositions can fit inside a day?

I research local midwives and read about C-sections elsewhere
  with no anesthesia   Babies left to die in incubators

They said *Never again*
  & here we are again   this time

  smoke-filled wind rushes from our pockets
Our palms hold microphones of grief

One moment   cries of a child missing a leg
  the next   leaders with mouthfuls of lies

Joe smiles holding ice-cream
  & inside me nausea rises

How to separate feelings of disgust
  from fecundity

My body falls into crevices of moments
My mind becomes spiderweb glistening dew of death

So much advice to not take in news
 but I judge everyone who chooses to turn eyes elsewhere

I cannot decide to mourn mass graves
  holding entire family lines

  anymore than I can elect to love music of the ocean

Thresholds

My sonogram says fourteen weeks
The journey moves faster than we realized
  and friend speaks to me about signs of clouds

  how she wishes someone had spoken to her about postpartum depression
  before her days crowded with storms
While my husband and I share a chocolate treat

  he speaks to me about mental health
  tells me how our friend talked to him about my tears
Love inspires so many fears of shadows

I melt into myself and no one tracks time
  how the first trimester hormones flow
  unbothered by decorum

I melt into myself and no one feels
  the divine soul download unfolding inside   how my body is a portal
an open door   a threshold stitching cosmos into bone

I melt into myself and no one sees my age
  how doctors use phrases like geriatric pregnancy
  to describe sacred work of my womb

I melt into myself and beloveds see
  woe but not its source
  no validation of the force wielded by The World

Every moment while I pick daisies   take shits
  play with my daughter
  new life sings alive inside me

Every day my phone greets me
  with brains spilling out of children's heads
  their legs kissed by meat grinders

  eyes of parents staring into mine
  like deafening vessels of ache
Tell me the appropriate response to a bouquet of different exhaustions

I am thirty-six chasing a toddler while pregnant
I am someone who refuses to look away
Eyes of loved ones judging grief

  only make the weight more
Is it depression or PTSD? What is second-hand trauma?
No pill will make me forget crimes of men with power

I don't need help before it's too late

                                                I only need what we all need
                  I take myself to the ocean   touch waves   pray

A Threading

> *"The Dungeness crab (Metacarcinus magister) makes up one of the most important seafood industries in the range it inhabits along the west coast of North America."* —Wikipedia

The first sentence in Wikipedia about *Metacarcinus magister*
  speaks of their usefulness to humans   how critical their meat to our economies

Common name from place of origin
Dungeness Spit   string of sand expanding fifteen feet per year

Weather   retrofits its moods
  while beaming singers sail in private jets

Oceans rise to meet rages of the day
  while fatigues turn to phoenix feathers

  because *All day (okay), I slay (okay), I slay (okay), I slay (okay)*
We gon' slay (slay), gon' slay (okay), we slay (okay), I slay (okay)

Every cup of Starbucks   an airstrike
Kites and children all fall down

  while elsewhere men stalk water for crabs
A man casts a net filled with hits of the '70s into air of Sooke Basin

He yells over his radio to make sure others know
  You gotta leave the girls!

A sign at the entrance elaborates
  All undersized crabs must be released immediately

The other dock is a flock of angry gulls

That's why fishing's great when it's fish!

It doesn't matter if it's big   small   male   female
You can take them all   as in   You can kill   them all

                Indiscriminately separate living beings from homes
                  Indiscriminately open entrails to sky

        I don't believe him   that indiscriminately is ever acceptable
        Most animals do not kill for pleasure   but humans   are special

                This is why we can't have anything nice
                    This is a story of The World

Soul of my soul   Reem
  my daughter   same pair of ponytails like ribbons on a breeze

Soul of my soul   my daughter
  brings Six of Cups and I wake up singing Mulan songs

Fond childhood memories covered in rubble
Overcoming a colonizing army   only permissible in cartoons

Disney is on a boycott list and I try to block out
  mornings crunching Frosted Flakes with siblings and a dragon

My daughter doesn't know creatures on endless immortal diapers
Let her know about the world that is   Let her imagine more than vibrant distractions

Give her vision of Octavia   June   Audre
Give her swords she will need to find ease we all deserve

                                                Resistance is justified
                                           when people are occupied

The least we can do is go screaming in the streets   wheatpasting   spray painting   blockading
  anything to wake up comfy neighbors

I tell my man *We suffer for those we love* and give him my eyes so he might feel my heart
My daughter hears my voice vibrato and I become soft moss

 honey and warm socks and sweet talk   pretend for a moment
 we live in time that makes smiling easy

She watches me swing between Manic   Panics
  pink-eyed clouds at sunset   seafoam green usnea

                                            Funny   how living beings of land
                                                and of oceans share shapes

                        Coral mushrooms   perfect replicas of bleached graveyards
                                        Veins like entanglements of vines

                    Mirrors   mirrors   everywhere
                      and still so many questions

            A pair of herons   great and blue holding court   courting
              across in-between space   that place where air meets water meets rock

        One faces west   One faces east
What are borders to wind   What are bodies to a soul

                        Made up   Temporary
                            Inconvenient

                Always some disturbance of scraped knees
                                        to say the least

                Always gotta be some talk about the economy
                        Billions of unbarreled oil off the shores of Palestine

Devices in our hands powered by cobalt
  mined by children paid in scarring of the lungs

In one place tiny fingers dig   In one place large fingers dig
                              bare hands

                          in sandals seeking treasure
chemical bonds used to end life   life surviving chemical bombs

We pay hundreds to take home packages
  warning of cancer and reproductive harm because

All day (okay), I slay (okay), I slay (okay), I slay (okay)
We gon' slay (slay), gon' slay (okay), we slay (okay), I slay (okay)

 myself and you and ourselves and each other
The hand planting a genocide gets veto power against its end

The starved able to walk leave bed to wait for flour
  while snipers wait for aid trucks to paint the ground red

                                     and   none   of   this   is   new
                   This is a story of the Earth

      Our moon looks on glad to only receive scraped knee of some flags
            without all the usual accompanying drama

Horror   Horror   Horror
  while some pull the trigger   some look away   some try to stop the gun

                    Which one are you?

                      Each bombed olive field is a threading together
                          asking we cast protest spells into wind

asking   that when we encounter someone who believes
       You can take them all

                    we find ways to live truth
      This is a story of myself and of you and of ourselves and of each other

DREAM FOR EARTH

A bald eagle watches a crow drum
  beak against plastic
  trying to access sweetness

Gulls perform a group piece
New shit!   Listen   the deep
  hums a different shade of sacred each moment

Dangerous levels of forever chemicals in ocean spray
  don't keep hands from touching water in reverence
  anytime a day has moments for a walk

I'm jealous of musicians
  when the tide rolls in
  against backdrops of fishing boats drifting across the harbor

These words will never recreate backwash aria
  collaging fist-sized rocks
  across kelp-lined coasts

Maybe if we hold hands
  we can make a song that's close
Ready?   *Breathe*   *Sing*

*

In second grade I found a small starfish
  took them home to a shoebox
  my mother filled with sand

It wasn't long before life left

Long legs dry   brittle
Little girl tears for a light that couldn't shine

  away from water
I am learning again what happens when we steal
Shield lichens and lungwort transform

  when forced to lounge on windowsills
Me and my daughter collect the shore in our pockets
  & colors become intertidal zones

Green splatter God painted across rock faces fades
A shade of seafoam or morning mist gray?
Who is to say?

Me and my husband bicker about colors
  of a chair   a cat   a coat
Our painter friend comes over

  & we always have some new reason to ask his opinion
Blue or black?   Black or brown?   Brown or red?
And   is a word almost able to describe internal waters

So many stories of beings
  part human   part Other
              shape dependent on place

What animal skin could I wear to turn me hopeful?
My daughter brings home a library book called *Be Here Now*
  to remind me of ways I fail at presence

I spew only craving and aversion
Enlightenment sounds like apathy
When I meditate the stillness only makes me more Scorpio

I ask america for love and receive black eyes
My country is an unkind lover who I leave
I watch the whole world mistreated

  and grieve bruises on other bodies
People thank me for social media posts
  and I cry that anyone could think so little is enough

I dream of guillotines
  while my womb sews together organs
Placenta passes nutrients   oxygen   plastic   rage

The day of the eclipse
  spiral wrack dances submerged
  an arm's length from dry feet

This place I thought so familiar
  with different jewels each visit
I always find what I am not seeking

In forests   ears strain to catch music of water
                                         Near water   I look for glimpses of forest
Maybe justice will appear if we stop searching far away from mirrors

Notes

The orb is a form originating in this book containing 24 lines in 8 tercets. The first word of each stanza becomes the last line of the next stanza. The final tercet has all seven repeated words in backwards order. The last word of all middle lines rhyme, and the last word is the first word in the poem—because I like the symbolism of circles.

"Orb: Forms of Worn Out" references a New York Times article and Dr. Anthony Fauci's prophecy about needless suffering and death if politicians failed to value lives over profit.

"Duplex" references Jericho Brown's dance between the ghazal and the sonnet.

"Patterns" includes lines from Genesis Chapters 6–8 of the Bible and references William Blake's "The Tyger."

"Frequently Asked Question" references the series of Frequently Asked Questions by Camille Dungy in *Trophic Cascade*.

"Hope is a Sweet Evening Sky Ripening" references the poem "'Hope' is the thing with feathers" by Emily Dickinson.

"Abecedarian Mango" references "Abecedarian Yellow" by Dan Vera and "Relax" by Ellen Bass.

"Searching for Mary Oliver & Always Finding Men" references the poem "The Summer Day" by Mary Oliver.

"Indoctrination" references the poem "Against the Police" by Miguel James.

"Ghazal for Abolition" references the introductory essay by Alexis Pauline Gumbs in *Revolutionary Mothering: Love on the Front Lines*. *Gumbs, Alexis Pauline, et al. Revolutionary Mothering: Love on the Front Lines, PM Press, Oakland, CA, 2016.

"An Astrology" includes lines from Genesis Chapters 37–42 of the Bible, and references *Citizen* by Claudia Rankine.

"They say I'm a beast" references the poem "Loose Woman" by Sandra Cisneros.

"Eye Gazing with Monsters" references Zora Neale Hurston's 1928 essay "How It Feels To Be Colored Me."

"Epithalamium" references the poem "I Loved You Before I Was Born" by Li-Young Lee.

"Remarks by President Biden on Recent Events on College Campuses / his truth in his lies" is an erasure of a speech Joe Biden gave on May 2, 2024.

"Girl, Bye (These Boots Are Made For Walking)" references the 1966 song written by Lee Hazlewood and performed by Nancy Sinatra.

The first stanza in "Fecundity" takes its definition from the Merriam-Webster dictionary.

"A Threading" includes lines from Beyoncé's song "Formation."

Acknowledgments

Praise be to God and all my ancestors for all the many blessings placed in my path. I know these poems and this beautiful life are only what they are because I do not walk alone. Thank you to the Earth, soil, and waters for showing me how to listen.

To Elliot, who said *This is your time to write*—thank you. Thank you for asking *Did you write today?* and *How did your writing go today?* and *Can I read what you worked on?* Thank you for being the best first reader, for asking questions, and for helping me to ask questions about the poems as they arrived. Thank you for all your encouragement. Thank you for holding me through all the hurt in this book and for inspiring so much joy. You helped this book come to life in so many ways.

Thank you to Neela and Luna—so many of the poems in this book would not exist without you.

Thank you to my parents for their love. My mother read to me every night when I was a child, going so far as to record her voice on an old-school tape recorder so that nights she worked as a nurse, all Miss Ivy had to do was push play for me to still fall asleep to my mother reading wherever we left off in our story. It was my mother who found Impressions Teen Magazine for me to volunteer at in middle school. My mother was the first person who read my poems starting way back in fourth grade—my biggest cheerleader. Mommy, you will always be part of why I am a writer.

To my Moon Sisters, Sophia Terazawa & Leah Tieger—thank you for all the ways you held me through the writing of this book. Thank you both for your thoughtful edits, your check-ins, and your hearts. Thank you to Ángel Faz for being an art sibling and conspirator of the soul. Thank you shō yamagushiku for grounding me in the spirit and in the work, for showing me what it means to be authentic and humble, and for listening to me cry and rant. Thank you to Jess Elwell, Lo Shrum, Aliya Schwab, Kai Mountfort, Jordyn Bonfonti, and Kim Walti for being good friends who gave me time to write by playing with my daughter. Truly—writing does not happen in isolation and is a labor of community.

Thank you to the writing communities that have so nourished me—this book would not be what it is without the relationships I formed in Anaphora, Corporeal Writing, and In Surreal Life. Thank you to the Hellbenders. Thank you to Aiyana Masala, and Danialie Fertile. Thank you to everyone in the ISL Afterlife who offered their thoughts and feedback.

Thank you to Will Evans—one of the most patient people on this planet. Thank you for the invitation to share these pieces of myself, for giving me the space to grow into these poems, and for all the support in so many ways over the years. Thank you to the entire team at Deep Vellum for bringing this book alive.

Many thanks to editors at the following journals who shared earlier versions of these poems:
  "Solidarity" (*Poetry Pause*)
  "Abecedarian Mango" (*Honey Literary*)
  "Youtubes My Mom Sends Me" (*Obsidian: Literature & Arts in the African Diaspora*)
  "March 2024" and "This Is The Soul Of My Soul" (*MAYDAY Magazine*)
  "Tornado Sirens When You Have A Sleeping Baby" (*Torch*)
  "Eye Gazing With Monsters" and "Orb: Climate Collapse Is Fucking Up My Birth Plan" (*sin Cesar*)
  "Anticipation" (*Elysium Review*)
  "Indoctrination" (*Rise Up Review*)

Thank you—you who read this right now—for being threaded together with me and with us all.

Katherine Tejada

Fatima-Ayan Malika Hirsi is a Black mother who spends time with forests and waters on unceded lands of the T'Sou-ke Nation. Her work strives to instigate action in service to world-building, social change, and collaboration.

www.ingramcontent.com/pod-product-compliance
Lightning Source LLC
Jackson TN
JSHW071525250825
89412JS00001B/1